# How Plants and Animals Live Together

## by May Evans

PEARSON
Scott
Foresman

DK

SO-CRQ-785

# What do plants and animals need?

Plants are living things.
Plants need air and water.
Plants need light from the Sun.
Plants need space.

Plants are producers.
A **producer** makes its own food.

Animals are living things too.
Animals need air and water.
Animals need shelter.
Animals need space.

Animals are consumers.
A **consumer** cannot make its own food.
A consumer gets food from its habitat.

# Different Needs

Plants and animals live together.
Plants and animals need each other.

Plants and animals get what they need from the places they live.

Big animals need a lot of food and space.
Small animals need less food and space.

If there is not enough food and space, some
animals may die.

# How do plants and animals get food in a grassland?

Most plants make food.
Some animals eat plants for food.
Other animals eat these animals.
This is a **food chain.**

All food chains start with the Sun.
Plants get energy from the Sun.
Plants use energy to make food.

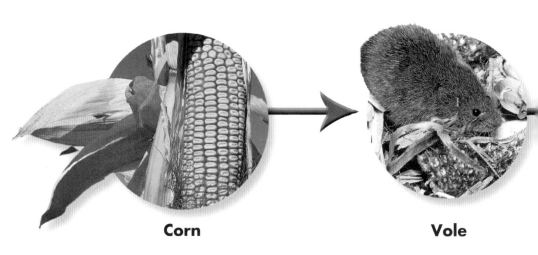

**Corn**                              **Vole**

Animals eat the plants and other animals.
Energy goes from the Sun to the animals.

All food chains have predators.
A **predator** hunts and eats other animals.

All food chains have **prey.**
Predators eat prey.
Prey is the food of predators.

**Coyote**                    **Mountain lion**

# Food Web in a Grassland

Places can have more than one food chain. A **food web** is many food chains in one place.

A grassland has many food chains. They make up a food web.

Raccoon

Corn

Vole

Fox

Look at the arrows in this food web.
How many animals eat corn?
How many animals eat voles?

Living things in a food web need each other for energy.

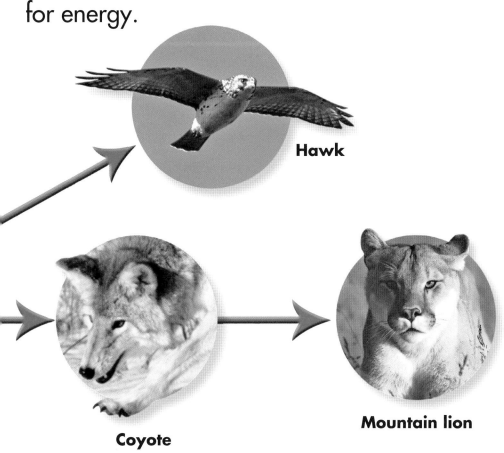

**Hawk**

**Coyote**

**Mountain lion**

# How do plants and animals get food in an ocean?

An ocean has food chains and food webs.

Kelp starts an ocean food chain.
Kelp grows in the ocean.
It uses light from the Sun to make food.

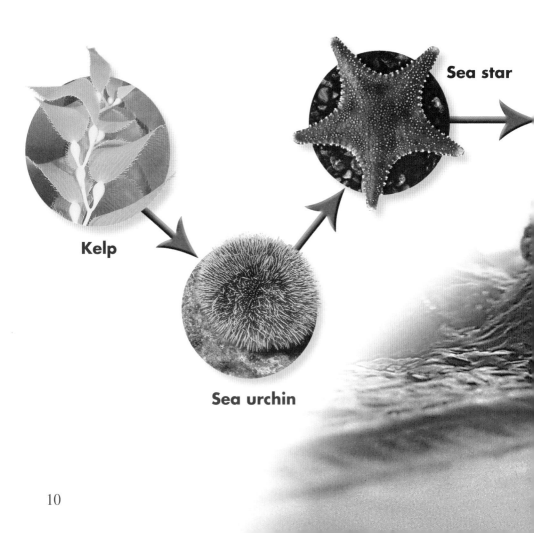

Kelp

Sea urchin

Sea star

The sea urchin gets energy when it eats the kelp.
The sea star gets energy when it eats the sea urchin.
Energy from the Sun goes to all the plants and animals in the ocean.

**Sea otter**

# A Food Web in an Ocean

There are many food chains in an ocean.
They make up ocean food webs.

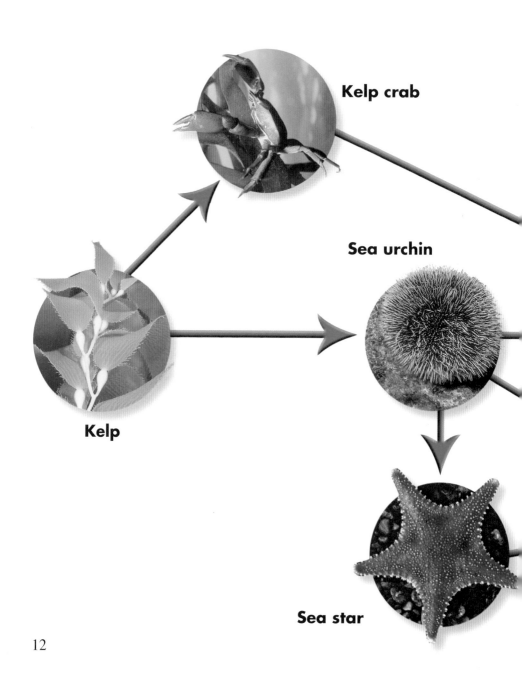

Kelp crab

Sea urchin

Kelp

Sea star

Look at this picture of an ocean food web.
Which animals eat kelp?
How many animals eat sea urchins?

**Orca**

**Sea otter**

**Sea gull**

# What can cause a food web to change?

Many things can change a food web.
Changes can hurt plants and animals.

Some changes are caused by people.
The oil from a ship spilled into the ocean.

Look at these sea otters.

Sea otters have fur.

The sea otters' fur was hurt by the oil.

People cleaned the sea otters.

They also cleaned the water.

People made the ocean safe again.

# How do plants and animals help each other?

Plants and animals can help each other.
Animals can use plants for shelter.
The animals can help the plants too.

An ant makes its home on an acacia plant.
The ant helps the plant stay safe.
It bites any animal that tries to eat the plant.

Cardinal fish live near sea urchins.
The sea urchin's spines stop other animals
from eating the fish.
Cardinal fish do not help or hurt the
sea urchins.

# Building Nests

Some animals use plant parts to make nests. Some animals use animal parts to make nests.

This squirrel's nest has twigs and leaves on the outside.
The twigs and leaves come from plants.
This nest has feathers and wool on the inside.
The feathers and wool come from animals.

# Animals Need Each Other

Sometimes animals help each other get food. Sometimes animals keep other animals safe.

This bird eats bugs that might hurt the rhino.

This boxer crab can stay safe near
a sea anemone.
A sea anemone is an animal.
The sea anemone can sting predators that
want to get the boxer crab.

A remora fish swims with a shark.
The shark keeps the remora fish safe.
It scares away predators.

The remora fish needs the shark.
The shark does not hurt the remora fish.

Plants and animals live together in their habitats.
They need each other in many different ways.

# Glossary

**consumer**    an animal that cannot make its own food but gets it from its habitat

**food chain**    how energy flows from the Sun to plants to animals in a habitat

**food web**    many food chains in one place

**predator**    an animal that hunts and eats other animals

**prey**    an animal that gets eaten by other animals

**producer**    a living thing that makes its own food